EL CAMINO ORACLE
Ancestral Wisdom for the Journey

by SABINA ESPINET

Copyright © 2022 U.S. Games Systems, Inc.

All rights reserved. The illustrations, cover design, and contents are protected by copyright. No part of this booklet may be reproduced in any form without permission in writing from the publisher, except by a reviewer who wishes to quote brief passages in connection with a review written for inclusion in a magazine, newspaper or website.

10 9 8 7 6 5 4 3 2 1

Made in China

Published by
U.S. Games Systems, Inc.
179 Ludlow Street
Stamford, CT 06902 USA
www.usgamesinc.com

INTRODUCTION

Walking in an immigrant's shoes is a precarious balancing act of navigating two worlds. It means having each foot planted in a different place and not completely belonging in either one, but knowing that you are supported by the richness of your ancestry. In Spanish, the word *camino* can be used to refer to a path, road, journey or the way. On their camino, immigrants carry the invisible baggage of traditions handed down through multiple generations, which gives them a well of ancient wisdom to draw from. They bear the weight of gratitude for the struggles of their predecessors and the responsibility for making the most of the opportunity that has been given to them. Because of this, they have ties to their past as well as a clear vision for the future.

My immigrant story begins in utero and is steeped in Caribbean and Hispanic roots. My camino began when my pregnant Trinidadian mother traveled from Canada to Colombia to give birth near her mother. The journey continued for the next decade as my father's occupation carried our family to several countries throughout South America. We eventually settled in a rural town in Florida where I felt excited yet very aware of how out of place I was. Sometimes, being an immigrant means hiding parts of yourself in an effort to adapt to a new environment.

Over time I grew more confident in my heritage, and instead of playing it down, I began reintegrating the different aspects of my dual nationality into my personality. The emotional journey of reconnecting with where I came from taught me how to embrace the wisdom of my elders and all that I bring to the table as a whole person. When we recognize the breadth of our cultural family tree, we give voice to our ancestors. We heal by bringing our shadow into consciousness and hopefully, we gain a deeper understanding of ourselves as individuals by learning to value what each of us has to offer the world. Through these cards you are invited to visit your past and celebrate your roots in order to live a more meaningful present and future.

Each of us goes on countless journeys of personal growth and development within the longer journey of our lifetime. With that in mind, El Camino Oracle has been crafted as a celebration of self-discovery, ancestry, diversity and the immigrant values that people of all nationalities inherently bring with them on their journey. We can apply these lessons to daily life and every new challenge. Although the point of view in the deck comes from personal experiences, you do not have to be Latinx or an immigrant to find meaning in the messages. Even those who don't know their biological family can become acquainted with their broader cultural family tree to find their ancestral guides. The principles depicted in this artwork are archetypes that are universal to our human experience and they bind us all to something greater. All of us are travelers—immigrants on this planet for the duration of our stay.

El Camino Oracle has 44 numbered cards loosely arranged to guide you through the stages of the proverbial hero's journey as defined by Joseph Campbell (Departure, Trials and Return). Some are serious, others playful, depending on what the situation or mood calls for. Each card has a title in both Spanish and English, which is also the keyword for the card. In Spanish, gender pronouns are used for words, but to avoid confusion I chose to keep the titles gender neutral. Each keyword is self-explanatory, but there is a corresponding story based on tradition, mythology or folklore from different countries to expand on the idea. These brief examples help to anchor you in the concept and maybe inspire you to dive deeper and learn more on your own. Both positive and negative sides are presented to hopefully remind you to think about your own journey with a kind and balanced perspective. Keep in mind that because of cultural diffusion, some of the examples may overlap with the traditions of nearby countries and are in no way meant to single out or exclude any particular place or group of people.

For the images, I chose symbols that encapsulated the theme of the card and best conveyed that emotion so that you can mentally carry it with you throughout your day. To emphasize the age and wisdom of these ideas, I used iconic Pre-Columbian imagery from South America and combined them with a rustic, folk art style of drawing. I mixed wet and dry media to give a rich texture and used vivid colors inspired by the traditional textiles and crafts of the region. I hope that all these elements come together and transport you to a place of curiosity and comfort, where you can safely explore your own customs and the path that you are on. Buen Viaje! (Safe travels!)

USING THE DECK

Experienced users know that how you care for and shuffle your cards is a personal choice. For newcomers, I have presented a few suggestions to get you started, but you are encouraged to make this journey your own. Creativity is welcome! Try to channel the celebratory spirit of Latinx culture in your practice by including all of the senses—play music, light a candle, burn incense, open the windows and let the natural elements in. Each card has a brief cultural anecdote to provide context and an asimilación (assimilation) prompt with questions or intentions to help you integrate these concepts and bring them into your daily life. For those who like working with inverted cards, the al revés (upside down) prompts ask questions to help determine what could be causing us to stumble on our path. They invite us to look at how our actions could be affecting our journey, without shame or judgment.

EL DIARIO (DAILY) GUIDANCE
— ONE-CARD DRAW —

This meditation focuses on goals or obstacles for the day. Spend a few moments visualizing what you hope to accomplish or overcome, then draw a card using whatever method comes naturally to you. Carry this image and message with you as you travel through your day.

LA BANDERA (THE FLAG) SPREAD
THREE-CARD DRAW

The Colombian flag is a symbol of independence from Spain, therefore this spread encourages you to look at your process of individuation. Choose three cards using the method you prefer and lay them side by side.

1. The first card (yellow) represents riches and the sun. What are your natural resources—the places you draw energy from and the people or things that make you feel rich in spirit?

2. The second card (blue) represents the sky and sea. How can you find renewal and refreshment for your soul?

3. The third card (red) represents sacrifice. What must you let go of to become more independent?

For a more meaningful and personalized experience, you are encouraged to adapt this spread to incorporate the colors and meanings from your country's (or organization or community) flag.

EL CAMINO SPREAD
FOUR-CARD DRAW

1	2	3	4
ORIGEN	CAMINO	OBSTÁCULO	DESTINO

This spread can be used to meditate on a long-term goal or during a new beginning, job, year or project. Select four cards and lay them out either horizontally or vertically to create a path.

- **CARD 1 • ORIGEN (ORIGIN)**
  What is keeping you from starting or what can you keep in mind during this starting point?

- **CARD 2 • CAMINO (PATH)**
  What do you need to carry with as you begin to take steps toward your goal?

- **CARD 3 • OBSTÁCULO (OBSTACLE)**
  What is holding you back or what reminders do you need as you face obstacles along the way?

- **CARD 4 • DESTINO (DESTINATION)**
  How can you honor how far you have come and recognize the work you put into arriving at your endpoint?

THE CARDS

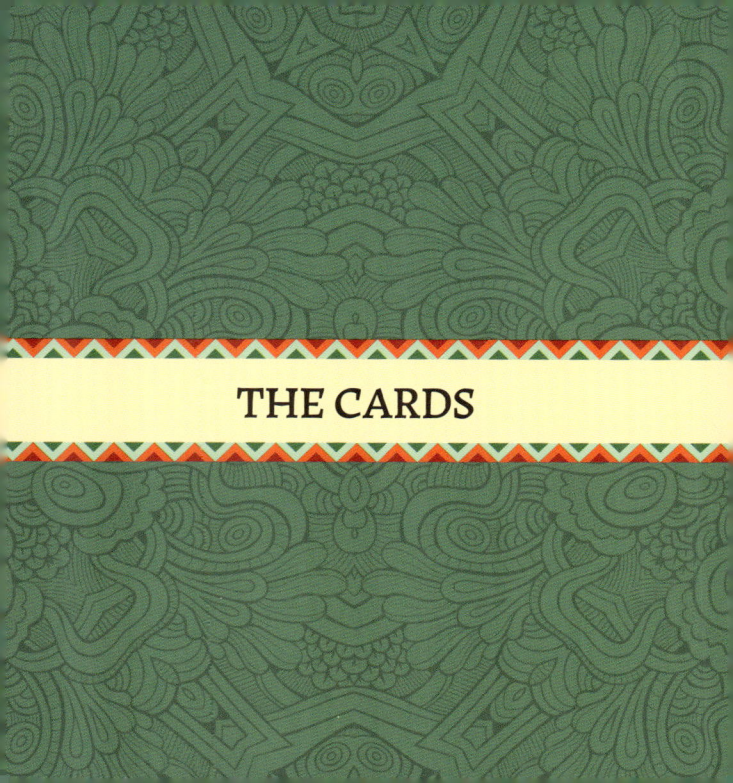

1 • CAMINO • JOURNEY

The Camino Inca (Inca Trail) is a 26-mile path that leads to Machu Picchu. The path was built to make pilgrimages on foot to the sacred site, sometimes carrying heavy loads. Today, people come from all over the world to make this high altitude, strenuous, four-day hike to follow in the steps of ancient people. Sometimes, walking the actual path of our ancestors and making a pilgrimage to a sacred place can remind us that we are not alone on the journey. It is a way to unite our physical and spiritual bodies and create a bond with our ancestors that transcends time.

Not every journey is epic, but each of us has a

personal quest to fulfill—what Joseph Campbell referred to as the hero's journey. Identifying our path is essential to our sense of purpose and also helps us to recognize when we stray from our path.

ASIMILACIÓN (ASSIMILATION)

"I choose to keep walking forward on my path."

What is the path you are called to be on? What is your personal quest? What steps are you taking today to stay on that path? Take a short walk, go on a hike or draw a map of your imagined journey.

AL REVÉS (UPSIDE DOWN)

Have you gotten distracted by something that doesn't help you along the way or have you strayed from your path? What are some ways that you can get back on track?

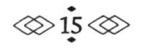

2 • ANCESTROS • ANCESTORS

The Muisca (or Chibcha) are one of the oldest tribes in South America. Long before the conquistadors and modern cities, they were living off of the land and thriving in large civilizations. They used tools, created beautiful pottery and made intricate ceremonial decorations and jewelry out of gold and gemstones.

Beyond our parents and grandparents, we carry the traditions, lessons, mistakes and successes of our elders within us. Our ancestors bequeath us with a rich inheritance of teachings if we only open ourselves to receiving their knowledge. By choosing to learn about our cultural origins, we gain a deeper understanding of ourselves and our history. We also have an opportunity to recognize the dark aspects and break violent cycles, repair damage and build upon the beautiful traditions of our lineage.

⬥ASIMILACIÓN (ASSIMILATION) ⬥

"I am not alone. The wisdom of my ancestors supports and guides me."

What can you learn from your ancestors? How can you honor their journey?

⬥ AL REVÉS (UPSIDE DOWN) ⬥

Are you silencing your ancestors' voices? Are you ignoring parts of your past?

3 ◆ RAÍCES ◆ ROOTS

South America is a continent rich with ancient raíces. Its oldest living tree is a living specimen of the largest species of tree found in South America, the Patagonian Cypress. This tree in Chile is over 3,600 years old—the second oldest tree in the world—named the Gran Abuelo Alerce (Great Grandfather Larch) by locals. It is considered a national landmark protected by the government and has survived logging, earthquakes and natural disasters.

Like the Gran Abuelo, we are rooted to the earth through our ancestors who create a vast root system that nourishes us. Truly learning about our past is not about romanticizing it and only identifying with the appealing parts. It also involves getting our hands dirty by digging in the proverbial dirt to acknowledge the painful aspects and learn life lessons. By recognizing the shadow in ourselves and our history, we can begin healing wounds.

ASIMILACIÓN (ASSIMILATION)

"My roots are deep, and my strength comes from all that I have survived."

Look at your life in perspective. Make a list of who or what keeps you grounded to the earth and notice how wide your branches spread. Reach out to one person with links you to your emotional, ancestral or symbolic roots.

AL REVÉS (UPSIDE DOWN)

How are you cutting yourself off from your roots? Have you been denying your ancient wisdom?

4 ◆ POTENCIAL ◆ POTENTIAL

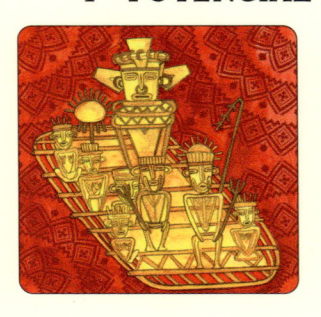

The legend of the mythical city of El Dorado (Golden One) originated when Spanish conquistadors heard rumors of a tribal chief of the Muisca people in Colombia who covered himself in gold dust and sailed on a raft making offerings of gold and jewels to the goddess in the Guatavita Lagoon. Over time, this story grew into a fable about a hidden city where all the buildings were made of gold. It sent many men on perilous quests in search of hidden treasures. Though the area has been explored many times and golden figurines have been retrieved from the lagoon, the actual city was never found.

Some say that it was a place indigenous people made up to fool and divert conquistadors away from their territory.

No matter where the truth lies, we can view El Dorado as a symbol of unfulfilled potential, a magical source within ourselves. We can choose to nurture our potential and attend to that source or deny its existence and cut ourselves off from the riches we have to offer.

◈ ASIMILACIÓN (ASSIMILATION) ◈

"My potential is an infinite source of inspiration and renewal."

How can you discover your hidden potential? What offerings can you make to this place?

◈ AL REVÉS (UPSIDE DOWN) ◈

Are you denying your potential or limiting yourself? Have you undervalued your inner treasure?

5 ◆ SUEÑOS ◆ DREAMS

A common dream for immigrants is for their children to be able to receive higher education. These aspirations begin as a sueño that is put into motion first with a plan, then through considerable sacrifice and effort, it can become a reality. Each of us has a dream but sometimes we are limited by economic, political or societal restrictions. Even so, the simple act of visualizing it can be the first step to help us start on the path to reach our destination.

Dreaming big is important. It gives us hope and a direction to aim toward. But the dream is only one part of the journey that launches us into action.

◈ ASIMILACIÓN (ASSIMILATION) ◈

"I commit to actively manifesting and visualizing my dreams and taking steps to make them come true."

Define your dreams. Get as detailed as you want; they can be short-term or long-term dreams. Once you have a starting point, list the steps that it will take to get to your destination.

◈ AL REVÉS (UPSIDE DOWN) ◈

How have you lost sight of your dreams? Or are you spending too much time dreaming and not taking action?

6 ◆ ESPERANZA ◆ HOPE

Eva Perón is immortalized in pop culture through the Andrew Lloyd Webber musical, *Evita.* Born in poverty, she rose to fame and became the first lady of Argentina and dedicated her life to being a champion for labor rights, women's suffrage and the poor. She was named the "Spiritual Leader of the Nation" by the government and is still a beloved symbol of hope and passion. It can be argued that hope is one of the strongest emotions that guide us on our journey because it motivates us to find the courage we need to fight for the potential of a better life.

Hope can be seen in the smiles of indigenous

children living in abject poverty and the tears of first generation immigrant parents watching their children graduate. It is a part of the human experience that each of us can access, but sometimes we need a symbol to remind us not to lose hope.

ASIMILACIÓN (ASSIMILATION)

"I make space for hope in my heart."

How or where can you find hope during challenging times? Look for role models who inspire you and make you feel hopeful.

AL REVÉS (UPSIDE DOWN)

How have you lost hope? What steps can you take to regain hope?

7 ✦ ESFUERZO ✦ EFFORT

The concept that dreams don't come true without effort is something immigrants are very familiar with. Uprooting your family and starting over in a strange environment requires an incredible amount of tenacity and determination. It takes hard work and dedication to form alliances, learn a new language and adapt to different cultural norms. They often take the lowest paying jobs cleaning, farming or doing manual labor to ensure that their children can succeed. Even those who have a degree might have to start over and get recertified in a new country to become licensed professionals. They understand that the payoff is almost always worth the risks and sacrifice, if not for them, then at least for the next generation.

Sometimes we can fall into a place of resentment over the work required to accomplish a task and want to look for shortcuts. In these moments, we can reflect on the kind of work our ancestors had to do and remind ourselves that we gain a sense of independence, satisfaction and pride from putting effort into creating something or finishing a project.

ASIMILACIÓN (ASSIMILATION)

"My relationships, values and goals require effort. I will work for what is important in my life."

What area do you need to put more work into? How can you take a risk to achieve a goal you have set for yourself?

AL REVÉS (UPSIDE DOWN)

Have you become lazy in the pursuit of creating a life that is meaningful to you? Are you putting effort into situations or relationships that are not in line with your growth and development?

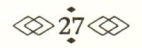

8 • RESISTENCIA • RESILIENCE

The famous Palenqueras are the colorful street vendors who sell their wares from large bowls or baskets carried on their heads. They were originally slaves who revolted from Spanish colonists and escaped to live in palenques (walled cities) in the jungles. They worked the land and began selling the fruit they picked to earn a living. Because of this resilience of spirit, they were able to fight for their independence and in doing so, rewrote their story to become a part of Colombian culture that is beloved by tourists and locals alike. Today, they are such a vital part of the culture that it has become a tradition for every crowned "Miss Colombia" beauty queen to pose for a photo with them.

It is easy to feel overwhelmed by circumstances in our lives and to forget that we have the power to change our story. Like the Palenqueras, we have the resilience of spirit and can overcome challenges and get back on our path.

◈ ASIMILACIÓN (ASSIMILATION) ◈

"I choose to use my inner power to find ways to be resilient instead of feeling victimized."

Think about the obstacles you face. How can you find innovative ways to fight for your independence and use what you have been given?

◈ AL REVÉS (UPSIDE DOWN) ◈

Have you given up? Are you letting your doubts debilitate you?

9 ◆ GANAS ◆ ENERGY

It took a lot of manpower to get that delicious coffee from the farm into your cup. Coffee plants are grown in the fertile, volcanic soil throughout Central and South America. These crops are temperamental and require just the right climate and a lot of maintenance. The delicate red fruit is hand-picked, then the seeds are manually separated before they are exported to be roasted all over the world and enjoyed at your local coffeehouse.

Like the caffeine in their daily tinto (black coffee), Latinx people are filled with energy. They talk fast, walk fast and get things done with ganas when it's time to work. But a little caffeine goes a long way! There are times we need this high-level energy and times when we should pay attention to whether we are moving too fast.

◈ ASIMILACIÓN (ASSIMILATION) ◈

"I will use my energy wisely today."

What can you put more energy into? Focus on this moment, on what needs to be done right now.

◈ AL REVÉS (UPSIDE DOWN) ◈

Have you felt lethargic about certain things in your life? Has your energy been depleted by people or situations that are toxic?

10 ◆ SACRIFICIO ◆ SACRIFICE

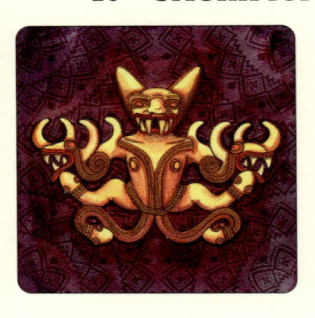

Bats play a significant role in South and Central American lore for many reasons, and because of this they are depicted on ceramics, masks and jewelry. Many ancient cultures such as the Aztec, Inca and Maya, performed human sacrifice rituals to honor and give thanks to their gods. Blood rituals were seen as a way to appease gods so that new life could continue, and because of their association to blood, bats became linked with sacrifice. The Maya even revered a vampire bat god, Camazotz. Seen literally, these are quite horrific and brutal acts of murder that seem savage to us now. Metaphorically, however, we can work with the idea of giving up something precious for the sake of a greater good. An act of selfishness that can transform and benefit us, our community, our family and our future, making way for something new.

Conversely, sacrificing ourselves in the service of a system that does not value our growth and oppresses us, is not a sustainable practice. For sacrifice to be a transformative experience, we have to be selective of who or what we put ahead of ourselves and consciously protect our health and mental well-being.

◈ ASIMILACIÓN (ASSIMILATION) ◈

"I choose to let go of situations, people and old patterns that don't support my growth."

What can you give up that is not serving you to bring about positive change in your life?

◈ AL REVÉS (UPSIDE DOWN) ◈

How have you sacrificed your own needs? Are you allowing yourself to be a victim?

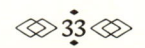

11 ♦ ADAPTABILIDAD ♦ ADAPTABILITY

The gauchos of Argentina were nomadic, mestizo horsemen who became popularized in folklore. Edgar Allan Poe wrote a poem about them and a style of pants named after them was a hot fashion item in the seventies. These men raised cattle and lived off of the land in the extremely harsh conditions at the rugged, southern tip of the continent. Identified by their traditional riding clothes that were practical and layered for warmth—hat, poncho, bandana and wide-legged riding pants—some version of these Hispanic vaqueros (cowboys) exists today in several countries. There are llaneros in Colombia and Venezuela, chalan in Peru and huaso in Chile.

These cowboys are a symbol of adaptability, grit and a will to beat the odds.

We are all capable of tapping into our own gaucho spirit and adapting to harsh conditions in order to survive. The challenge is not becoming hardened by the bitter aspects of life.

ASIMILACIÓN (ASSIMILATION)

"I am open to the flow of life and know I can adapt to survive the challenges ahead."

What are some ways that you have adapted? How can you learn from those situations as you face roadblocks in your day or life?

AL REVÉS (UPSIDE DOWN)

Are you too rigid in your outlook or afraid of change? What can you do to allow yourself to be more fluid or open-minded?

12 ♦ VALOR ♦ COURAGE

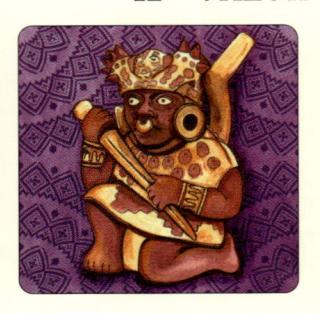

This card for valor depicts a pottery relic of a warrior from the Moche tribe. "No one leaves home unless home is the mouth of a shark" wrote Warsan Shire in her poem, "Home." It takes great courage to undertake a new journey. The narrative that all immigrants have a choice to leave their country is convenient, but the reality is that many are seeking asylum and refuge from dire conditions. They risk their lives by staying and also by leaving and are sometimes forced to endanger their children for a chance at their long-term safety.

Fortunately, most of us will never have to face such heartbreaking choices, but courage is a survival instinct that each of us has inherited from our ancestors. When faced with life's most trying circumstances, we can imagine the courage they had to summon to hunt dangerous beasts, live in the wilderness and travel long distances for a better life. Their courage can be a source of strength to guide us.

ASIMILACIÓN (ASSIMILATION)

"I am not alone and will not let fear guide me."

Think about situations where you, your parents or grandparents had to find courage. Where can you find courage when you feel frightened?

AL REVÉS (UPSIDE DOWN)

Are you experiencing false courage or bravado that is keeping you from growing or learning?

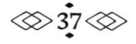

13 ◆ ORGULLO ◆ PRIDE

The indigenous Cholita women of Bolivia were once treated as second class citizens. The pejorative name, Chola, was given to them by the Spaniards. Tales were told about their poor hygiene and they were banned from walking through wealthy neighborhoods and shooed away from some public areas. Recently, these women have started to reclaim their stature and proudly showcase their eclectic style. Their colorful layered skirts, richly embroidered laramas (shawls), decorative jewelry and braided hairstyle topped with their trademark borsalinos (bowler hats) make up an undeniably original look. There are even groups of Cholas breaking down feminine stereotypes such as the popular female wrestlers called, "Cholitas Luchadoras" (The

Fighting Cholitas) and the mountain climbing "Cholitas Escaladoras" (climbing cholitas). Cholas have learned to market their look and have empowered themselves to become savvy business owners and an emblem of Bolivia's indigenous people.

Becoming too prideful about the wrong things can leave us feeling empty. Authentic pride does not come from money or fame, but from within. It can shine through in how we carry and care for ourselves and what we choose to nurture and feed.

ASIMILACIÓN (ASSIMILATION)

"I am proud of who I am at this moment."

What are some things you are proud of about yourself? How can you showcase your best attributes or personal accomplishments?

AL REVÉS (UPSIDE DOWN)

Have you become inflated? Is your pride getting in the way of you living fully and authentically?

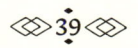

14 ✦ AMOR ✦ LOVE

Latinx culture is overflowing with symbols of love! From the heart-shaped philodendron leaves to the Peruvian Lilies that symbolize devotion, and the red Hibiscus that represents romantic love. In popular culture there is the "Latin lover" stereotype and in literature there are many classic tales of love such as *Don Quixote de La Mancha* and *Love in the Time of Cholera*. But perhaps, the most famous modern personification of love is Walter Mercado, the Puerto Rican astrologer and TV personality. Walter was known for his daily sign-off, "Con mucho, mucho, mucho amor!" (With lots and lots and lots of love!) He said that the reason he wore flamboyant costumes was to attract attention so that more people would hear his message of love above all. By fanatically and unapologetically spreading this message, he became an international icon and cultural phenomenon. Walter reminded us daily to love one another and that love is the most important thing.

Choosing love does not mean denying that the dark side of life exists or failing to recognize when we witness hate. Instead, we can look for love around us and actively transform the world with the way we think, speak and act towards ourselves and others.

◈ ASIMILACIÓN (ASSIMILATION) ◈

"I am love. I choose love."

What are some ways that you can love yourself and others? Tell someone you love them. Remind yourself that you are loved.

◈ AL REVÉS (UPSIDE DOWN) ◈

How are you denying yourself the love that you deserve?

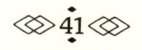

15 ✦ HOSPITALIDAD ✦ HOSPITALITY

Pineapples originated in Brazil and have become a symbol of hospitality throughout the world, which is a reflection of the welcoming spirit of Latinx culture. It can be felt in the greeting, "Bienvenido! Mi casa es su casa." (Welcome! My home is your home.) From an early age, children are taught to be gracious hosts and that there is always extra food and a place at the table for unexpected guests. Neighbors are looked after, gifts are given, doors are always open and everyone is greeted with warm embraces and cheek kisses.

Having a place where we belong is important to our sense of self and emotional well-being. Unfortunately, immigrants are not always made to feel welcome in their new homes. Finding the balance between making others feel welcome while having healthy boundaries, can be a healing and rewarding form of human bonding.

◈ ASIMILACIÓN (ASSIMILATION) ◈

"I open my heart to being more accepting to myself and inclusive of others."

Where do you feel most welcome? How can you be more hospitable to others? Nurture your kind-hearted spirit by making a small donation to a local food bank or immigrant shelter. Smile at a stranger, visit a nursing home or deliver baked goods to a neighbor.

◈ AL REVÉS (UPSIDE DOWN) ◈

How have you been closed off or unwelcoming? Being accommodating or generous without limits can be harmful. Where do you need to establish healthy boundaries?

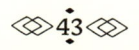

16 ✦ COMUNIDAD ✦ COMMUNITY

The indigenous Wayúu people live in the desert peninsula of Colombia and Venezuela. They coexist in matriarchal groups, earning a living by selling woven goods that have become trendy fashion accessories. Women run the households and the businesses; men primarily raise goats and build shelters. The Wayúu sense of community is similar to immigrant groups. Because of their struggles, they eagerly help others in similar situations. They recognize that security comes from safety in numbers and that a shared load will be lighter. They also tend to support businesses that operate in their close-knit neighborhoods.

Humans are social creatures and benefit from group connections, where we can assist each other and receive support. For community to truly work, there must be a symbiotic relationship. When we become isolated, it is easier to dehumanize entire groups of people and forget that we are all one. Community extends beyond our immediate family and can be found with our neighbors, found family, colleagues, faith groups and online special interest groups. And of course, when we feel isolated, we can remember that we are always supported by the community of our ancestors.

ASIMILACIÓN (ASSIMILATION)

"I am a valuable part of a vast network of people who rely on me and whom I can rely on."

It's okay to lean on others for support and ask for help. Who is part of your community? How can you support others?

AL REVÉS (UPSIDE DOWN)

Have you become isolated or separated from others? Do you not ask for help or give help to others?

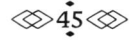

17 ✦ PADRE ✦ FATHER

Simón Bolívar, "El Libertador" (The Liberator), is hailed as one of the greatest heroes of the South American independence movement and is considered to be the founding father of many countries. During his short life, he fought in over one hundred battles against the Spaniards and helped liberate Bolivia, Colombia, Ecuador, Panama, Peru and Venezuela and worked to establish a union of independent Latin countries.

When channeled, masculine energy can be a healthy and productive component of our individuation that aids us in accomplishing great things. Unbalanced, it can turn into an exaggerated sense of male pride. This machismo has long been associated with Latinx men and has done much to injure the environment, women and the LGBTQ+ community. Throughout Latinx countries the gender equality gap is wide, and aggression toward women is high. On our journey, there are times when our masculine energy is deficient and other times when we need to access it—the key is learning to understand what the situation calls for.

◈ ASIMILACIÓN (ASSIMILATION) ◈

"I choose to use my drive and ambition positively to support my independence and growth."

How can you use your positive father energy and assert your autonomy in your speech and actions? Is there a positive father figure in your family or your culture you can look to for leadership?

◈ AL REVÉS (UPSIDE DOWN) ◈

Are you falling prey to antiquated patriarchal viewpoints that are holding you back from your independence?

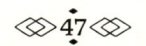

18 ◆ ABUELA ◆ GRANDMOTHER

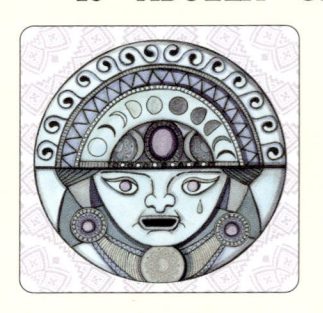

Mama Killa (Moon Mother) was the Incan great mother figure who protected women and was the goddess of the moon, marriage and the menstrual cycle. Her tears were said to turn into the silver that was mined from the mountains. A modern version of Mama Killa is the abuela, the iconic central figure who holds the family together in Latinx culture. Abuelas are imperfect and they don't do anything extraordinary. They are simply there—cooking, singing, praying, telling stories—a steady and constant example and source of comfort, nurturing, discipline and acceptance. Through them, we absorb affection, learn feminine traditions and family values and are supported by the matriarch.

When we cut ourselves off from the great mother energy–as individuals and as a collective–it creates an imbalance in the system that can be very harmful. Including and integrating her helps us achieve wholeness.

ASIMILACIÓN (ASSIMILATION)

"The matriarch watches over me and guides me. I open myself to her care and wisdom."

To feel the love of abuela, there is nothing you need to do, just open your heart.

AL REVÉS (UPSIDE DOWN)

How have you ignored the feminine guidance in your life? Can you find a positive feminine role model in your family or culture that reminds you of abuela?

19 ◆ LUZ ◆ LIGHT

Since our origin, human beings have been celebrating light. The Muisca and Inca worshipped the sun gods, Sué and Inti. In modern times, light is still an important part of our rituals. The Dia de las Velitas (Day of Candles/Light) is celebrated in Colombia to mark the Immaculate Conception of Mary. On this evening, thousands of votive candles are lit in paper lanterns on sidewalks, porches, balconies and town squares. It is an amalgamation of Catholic and indigenous traditions as well as colonists' belief that the light from torches protected people by keeping panthers away.

Since the dawn of man, light has brought us

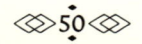

comfort. It helps our food grow, gives us energy and illuminates the way. A little bit of light can help us when we feel lost and feel unsafe in the darkness.

⬦ ASIMILACIÓN (ASSIMILATION) ⬦

"My inner spark illuminates the world."

Light a candle to remind yourself to shine your unique and vibrant light into the world.

⬦ AL REVÉS (UPSIDE DOWN) ⬦

Where do you feel that you need more light in your life? Are you surrounding yourself only with darkness?

20 ◆ FE ◆ FAITH

The Inca built temples to their god Viracocha, who created the universe. They worshipped and observed the stars because they believed the constellations were interconnected with everything and affected their agricultural cycles. In modern times, we continue to look for symbols and build monuments to faith. The Andean (Incan) Cross dates back to 300 BC. Its symmetrical shape incorporates the four cardinal directions and seasons. In the last century it has been renamed Chakana and has become a symbol of Incan faith and values. Throughout South America there are many monuments to faith, including the Christ the Redeemer statue in Brazil, and the Salt Cathedral of Zipaquirá built into a salt mine in Colombia.

Faith is a principle that immigrants must carry on their camino. It can be a specific religious belief or a source within that keeps them moving forward when all seems lost. The idea of something greater than ourselves that protects us during trying times can be comforting. Ultimately, faith can be found within our own hearts, but sometimes we need concrete markers along the way to remind us of our beliefs. When we lose our faith, we lose our sense of direction on our journey. Visiting a sacred place can help recalibrate our way forward.

⬦ ASIMILACIÓN (ASSIMILATION) ⬦

"I believe in _____"
(List three personal core principles)

What do you believe in that helps you feel supported? Is there a place you can go to feel more in touch with your belief system?

⬦ AL REVÉS (UPSIDE DOWN) ⬦

Have you lost faith? How or where can you look for faith?

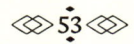

21 ◆ BENDICIÓNES ◆ BLESSINGS

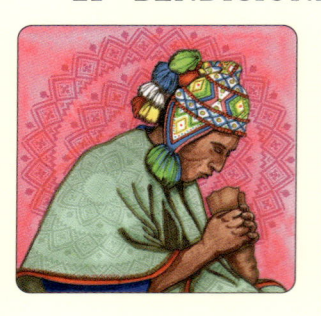

Blessings are an integral part of the Latinx language and culture. From the Andean high priests who perform despacho ceremonies (blessing rituals) in the mountains, to a layperson offering bendiciónes when they answer the phone, part ways or close written correspondence. Parents almost always verbally bless their children at the end of every call or visit. This practice is not associated with any particular religion, but with a desire to extend protection and good health to loved ones.

We have the power to manifest abundance or scarcity depending on our mindset. When we incorporate bendiciónes into our daily routines, we are choosing to acknowledge the boundless source of abundance and to generously share it with others.

⬦ ASIMILACIÓN (ASSIMILATION) ⬦

"I am grateful for this heartbeat, this breath and this moment. I choose to see the abundance in life."

Count your blessings. Train yourself to notice the abundance around you and to be open to receiving blessings. Practice making your first and last thoughts of the day thoughts of gratitude.

⬦ AL REVÉS (UPSIDE DOWN) ⬦

Have you been focusing only on the negative or scarcity? Are you comparing yourself to others? Instead of focusing on what's missing, think about what you have right now.

22 ◆ PROTECCIÓN ◆ PROTECTION

Throughout Latin America, Catholicism is the predominant religion, often imbued with rituals from indigenous people and slaves. A person can be simultaneously very religious yet also superstitious. There are lots of protection rituals such as burning Palo Santo (holy tree) wood or wearing black jet to ward off mal ojo (evil eye). In Venezuela, carrying a peccary tooth is thought to bring protection and good luck. Another way to ask for protection is by displaying milagros (miracles), the wooden hearts or crosses with tiny, hammered tin charms. Each charm represents something you are asking to be protected.

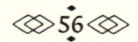

We all have a basic need to feel safe and protected. This is especially true for immigrants, since they face dangers during their travels and in unfamiliar environments. We can't stop tragic things from happening, but carrying a little amulet or having a protection ritual can provide a sense of comfort. But fear can cause us to over-protect ourselves and our loved ones. Finding a balance and learning to trust takes time and daily practice.

ASIMILACIÓN (ASSIMILATION)

"I trust that I am protected and watched over by the love of my ancestors."

Find a tiny amulet or charm to carry in your purse, wallet or pocket to remind you that you are protected. Touch this object if you are feeling fearful. What other small things can you do to feel protected in your home and in relationships?

AL REVÉS (UPSIDE DOWN)

Have you been letting fear lead you? What choices or thoughts have caused you to feel unsafe? Remind yourself, "I have everything I need at this moment. I am protected."

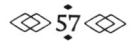

23 ◆ MEDICINA ◆ MEDICINE

Curanderos–indigenous healers in the Amazon and Andean regions–have a vast array of algae, roots, herbs and fruit at their disposal. Over generations, they have learned to work with these ingredients, found nowhere else on earth, in ways we may not understand. For centuries, indigenous people throughout the Andean region have used leaves from the coca plant to help with altitude sickness and digestion. Today, Mate de Coca is a tea commonly used to provide a light energy boost similar to coffee and many medicinal benefits. In Bolivia, a traditional indigenous cure uses lizards to help mend fractures and broken bones. The lizards are soaked in herbs and alcohol, chopped and blended into a paste that is applied to the injury and bandaged with newspaper for several days. This may sound exotic and even repulsive to most people, but some claim the cure is effective.

We tend to dismiss and be skeptical of practices that seem strange to us. But there is value in considering alternative natural remedies. If we keep an open mind, we can work with the medicine of our ancestors to heal our bodies and minds.

◈ ASIMILACIÓN (ASSIMILATION) ◈

"I choose to put my mental and physical health first."

How can you learn healing practices from your ancestors? How can you take better care of your health?

◈ AL REVÉS (UPSIDE DOWN) ◈

Are you ignoring your health or the wisdom of your physical body? How are you causing injury to yourself?

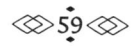

24 ◆ SUERTE ◆ LUCK

On New Year's Eve, Colombians eat twelve grapes with each bell chime at midnight to bring prosperity during each month of the coming year. In Peru, a tumi (ceremonial Incan knife) is hung on walls for good luck. In several countries, it can also bring bad financial luck to put your purse on the floor–draining you of wealth. And if you are a single woman who wants to get married, never let someone sweep over your feet!

These practices are small reminders that we do not have control over what the future brings, but we can put positive thinking into practice and actively welcome and manifest good fortune into our daily lives.

⬖ ASIMILACIÓN (ASSIMILATION) ⬖

"I welcome prosperity and abundance into my life."

What is an object that you are drawn to for luck? Display it prominently in your home or workspace. Look around your daily life for symbols of luck as reminders to think positively.

⬖ AL REVÉS (UPSIDE DOWN) ⬖

How are your negative thoughts preventing you from accessing good luck?

25 ◆ BROMISTA ◆ TRICKSTER

The trickster is an important player in every cultural mythology, and it is no different in Caribbean and Latin American countries. There are countless examples of jokers such as the anteater from Ecuador that trades skin with a jaguar or the female turtle trickster in Colombia who outsmarts animals and uses their bones as musical instruments.

Tricksters are neither good nor bad. They serve to shake up the status quo and challenge deities or traditional beliefs, frequently by using humor and ridicule. They overcome obstacles using wit and they embarrass antagonists with their pranks. In doing so, they teach us to not take ourselves, and life, too seriously and bring balance by showing us our imperfections and weaknesses.

◈ ASIMILACIÓN (ASSIMILATION) ◈

"I can look for the humor in situations that challenge me."

How can you bring balance to a situation by seeing the humor in it? How can you work with the trickster energy in your life to learn to laugh at yourself and challenge the status quo? Find out how the trickster shows up in the mythology of your culture, or one you are interested in.

◈ AL REVÉS (UPSIDE DOWN) ◈

Are you taking yourself too seriously? Have you forgotten how to use wit and ingenuity in difficult situations?

26 ◆ BRUJERÍA ◆ WITCHCRAFT

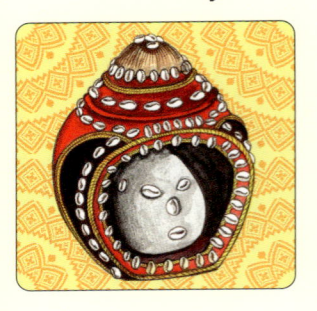

Over the centuries, many women throughout the Americas were tried as witches by colonial inquisitors because they were said to brew bewitched chocolate drinks and love potions. Throughout history, witchcraft has been presented as something to be feared, when in reality so much of it is harmless and simply comes from the spiritual beliefs of nature-worshipping indigenous and African people. Santería, for example, is a religion based on Yoruba traditions brought to Caribbean and South American countries by West African slaves. Christians feared these rituals so much that for decades Santería was banned in places and had to be practiced in secret, giving it further association with the occult.

Just because a behavior is different or we don't understand it, doesn't mean we should fear it. Viewing unusual practices from another perspective helps us to grow and expand our way of thinking.

◈ ASIMILACIÓN (ASSIMILATION) ◈

"I choose to maintain an open mind and attitude."

What is unknown to you that causes fear? How can you learn about it or from it?

◈ AL REVÉS (UPSIDE DOWN) ◈

How are you letting fear keep you from learning?

27 ◆ RETABLO ◆ ALTAR

Altars are found in churches of course, but often Latinx families have retablos or nichos (small decorative altars) in their homes as well. They were introduced by priests who brought statues of saints in small boxes with them from Spain to help convert indigenous people. These miniature devotional spaces can include a painting or small figure of a saint and are decorated with jewels and painted flowers. Offerings such as candles, holy water, incense, money, food or even a little shot of liquor can be given. They are living vignettes, personalized and maintained with great respect and regularly refreshed.

Deciding what we will and won't give our devotion to can be a mindful way of directing our energy. Creating a space for reverence is a joyful way of prioritizing and defining what is meaningful to us.

◈ ASIMILACIÓN (ASSIMILATION) ◈

"I make space for reverence in my heart."

Create an altar space in your home using a shelf or decorative box and personalize it with sentimental or special objects that are sacred to you. Set aside time to visit and dust your altar regularly. What literal and metaphorical offerings can you make to your altar?

◈ AL REVÉS (UPSIDE DOWN) ◈

What area of your life have you forgotten to pay respect to?

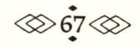

28 ✦ RECUERDO ✦ KEEPSAKE

The Spanish word recuerdo translates literally to "remember." Immigrants bring objects with them to keep the memory of their country of origin and family alive. Keeping a sentimental book, rosary or an item of jewelry or clothing is a way of carrying our ancestors with us on our journey. These personal objects have an energetic memory and holding or using an item that a loved one touched is a way to be tangibly connected with them through time. Our deceased relatives remain in our hearts and minds no matter what, but through family heirlooms, we can be reminded that we are supported by them.

Collecting objects with special meaning can help deepen our relationships with our ancestors. Likewise, placing value primarily on material things and focusing only on accumulating wealth, can be a distraction from what really matters.

ASIMILACIÓN (ASSIMILATION)

"I hold this object to remind me that you are always walking by my side."

What objects remind you of a person who loves you? Hold them in moments of fear or uncertainty.

AL REVÉS (UPSIDE DOWN)

Are you placing value in things that don't support you? Have you forgotten what is important to you?

29 ✦ MUERTE ✦ DEATH

Death appears frequently in Latinx culture, the most popular instance being the Mexican Dia de Los Muertos (Day of the Dead) holiday when family members cook meals and decorate altars and cemeteries to honor their deceased. The Colombian legend of La Llorona (the weeping woman) is about a ghost who walks the streets crying in perpetuity for her dead children and the story has even been made into a horror movie. And during the Colombian Carnaval, dancers reenact a battle between life and death in a dance called La Danza del Garabato, in which a man battles the grim reaper.

Death is ever present—it marks the end, but also

an opportunity for a new beginning. We can't escape the inevitability of it, so why not embrace it and find ways to learn to accept it as part of life?

◈ ASIMILACIÓN (ASSIMILATION) ◈

"I accept that this ending is a part of life, not a punishment."

How can you acknowledge the cycle of life and mark an ending (in a relationship, job, or phase of life)?

◈ AL REVÉS (UPSIDE DOWN) ◈

What are you keeping alive that might be time to let die?

30 • PESAR • GRIEF

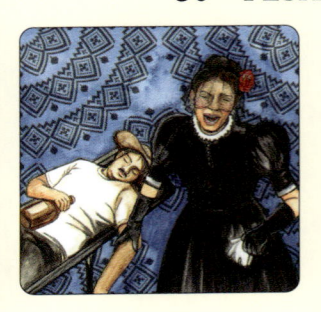

To mark the final day of the Carnaval de Barranquilla there is a parade for Joselito Carnaval. The story goes that he was a coach driver who celebrated and imbibed so much during Carnaval that he died from partying too much and went "de la rumba, a la tumba" (from the party to the grave). To honor him, on the day before Lent, a man on a stretcher or in a coffin is carried through the streets to represent the death of Joselito, the spirit of Carnaval. Grieving widows and mourners dramatically wail and cry out, "Joselito se murió!" (Joselito has died!) as the processions parade through town. It is a light-hearted reminder that life is short and should be enjoyed, but all good things must come to an end.

Unlike death, grief is not a final state, but a process that we must move through. Acknowledging our pain allows us to let go of the past, of old relationships that don't benefit us, of old hurts, of memories or loved ones. A healthy amount of grief can open us up to the next phase of life.

ASIMILACIÓN (ASSIMILATION)

"I mourn this loss and honor the lessons it has taught me."

Physically mark your grief: cry, laugh, tear up old photos, draw a picture or write a letter and burn it. It is important to express the feelings so that you don't become stuck on your journey.

AL REVÉS (UPSIDE DOWN)

Is your grief consuming you and keeping you from moving on?

31 ◆ NATURALEZA ◆ NATURE

Our environment is part of us on a deep, cellular level. Madremonte and Pachamama are two of the Mother Nature figures that are predominant in South American folklore. They watch over the jungles and animals and have power over the weather and vegetation. Fiercely protective of the natural realms, they can cause people to get lost in the wilderness and are known to punish poachers, fishermen and hunters.

Recently we have witnessed in horror as animals and indigenous people in the Amazon, the lungs of our planet, have been displaced by deforestation and fires. We are all one interconnected ecosystem and when we forget that and become detached from the natural world, there is a high cost that we all pay.

◈ ASIMILACIÓN (ASSIMILATION) ◈

"I am a part of the natural world and the natural world is a part of me."

We can get in touch with nature, even in the city. Step outside, inhale the scents, listen to the sounds, look at the clouds or feel the wind. If you can, touch water or hold a rock, leaf or feather. Take a moment to simply sit with nature and think about how to carry that feeling with you when you feel unsupported. Find a print or photograph of nature from your country and display it.

◈ AL REVÉS (UPSIDE DOWN) ◈

Have you become detached from the natural world? What are the consequences of that detachment? How can you help stop the damage?

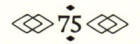

32 ♦ COMIDA ♦ FOOD

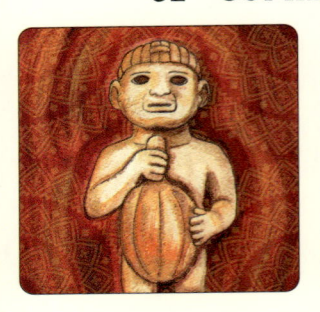

The next time you are enjoying a chocolatey treat, thank your Latinx friends. The cacao tree originated in the Amazon basin, then was domesticated over 4,000 years ago by the Mayan people and used to make ceremonial chocolate drinks. Sharing meals is a human gesture that unites us on a primitive level, and it can be one of the first ways to understand a person or a community. In every culture, food is the most instinctual way of bonding. Preparing and sharing meals is a powerful way to communicate through regional flavors and ingredients and to show mutual respect by experiencing the giving and receiving of nourishment.

Often immigrants make and sell their culinary specialties as a means to earn a living in a new country. By sharing their cuisine, they are creating a source of income for themselves and also sharing a part of their heritage.

⬧ ASIMILACIÓN (ASSIMILATION) ⬧

"I can nourish and comfort my soul in healthy ways."

"Buen provecho!" (Enjoy your meal!) Eat or share food from your culture–a slice of fruit, a dish using spices, or a typical drink. Think about how you can nourish your soul more.

⬧ AL REVÉS (UPSIDE DOWN) ⬧

What area of your life needs more nourishment? How can you feed it?

33 • IDIOMA • LANGUAGE

Many indigenous languages have been lost through the ages, and with them a way of understanding our past. One of the few survivors is Quechuan, the language of the Incan people and the most widely spoken Pre-Columbian language in South America. It is still spoken by a large population of Peruvians and is an important part of the country's heritage that is actively being preserved and passed on to new generations.

We all have a voice and a right to be heard. Recently, minga protests have been organizing in Colombia and Ecuador. The word minga is of Quechuan origin and describes traditional gatherings to benefit the common good. In these protests, thousands of indigenous people have come together to use their language and voice to demand justice –for their rights and issues to be heard by the government. Our spoken words are powerful and help us to understand one another. They can also cause harm and divide us depending on how we choose to use them.

ASIMILACIÓN (ASSIMILATION)

"My words matter, and I can choose how to use them."

Think about how you communicate and what you are saying. What is the language of your ancestors? Can you learn a few words or a phrase from their language to communicate with them?

AL REVÉS (UPSIDE DOWN)

How can you communicate more clearly and effectively? Have you been silent? How can you speak up more or speak out against ideas that you disagree with?

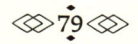

34 ◆ CUENTOS ◆ STORIES

Oral tradition is a way of preserving history, folklore, traditions and recipes. Through these cuentos told from memory, elders can teach specific skills such as weaving. For example, the sombrero vueltiao (turned hat) has been made by hand through an elaborate process handed down through word of mouth for generations. Making these hats requires many steps and each part is taught to a different person in the family, who then becomes specialized in that particular technique. These stories enable villagers to keep their culture alive, creating an economic opportunity that gives families a sense of pride and Colombians a symbol of their identity.

Understanding who we are allows us to share our unique gifts with confidence. Learning our stories and telling them, helps us to shape and strengthen our identity. When we don't take the time to get to know ourselves, we can feel hollow and look to others to adopt their identity.

ASIMILACIÓN (ASSIMILATION)

"I can live more fully in the present when I know the stories of my past."

Reflect on your particular story and the experiences you have had along the way. Share your stories.

AL REVÉS (UPSIDE DOWN)

Have you forgotten your story—your values, knowledge and identity? No one else can tell your story. You can choose to be the hero in your story, rather than the victim.

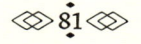

35 ◆ TEJADOS ◆ TEXTILES

In Peru, chullo hats were originally made by the Andean people from local alpaca wool to keep their ears covered and warm, but they have become a hip accessory worn around the world. Colombia is also known for its exquisitely woven chinchorros (hammocks) and mochillas (tote bags). Each unique weaving or knitting technique varies from country to country and even within specific villages, making the finished pieces not only practical, but also regional identifiers. Creating textiles usually involves most members of the family and can be a source of income for entire towns. The styles, patterns and dyeing methods are passed on through generations, creating a link through the ages.

Textiles tell multi-layered stories. When we hold handmade fabrics, we are not only witnessing the craftsmanship of a single person but the collective efforts of a family, a village, a culture—the literal tapestry of our heritage.

◈ ASIMILACIÓN (ASSIMILATION) ◈

"The fabric of my life is strong because it is woven with the threads of my ancestors."

How can you weave your ancestors and culture into your daily life? Can you purchase a small woven item from your culture to remind you of the ancestral threads that run through you?

◈ AL REVÉS (UPSIDE DOWN) ◈

Has the fabric of your soul become frayed? Is there an area of your life that needs mending?

36 ♦ MÚSICA ♦ MUSIC

Every country has its unique sound defined by the instruments developed from the materials of their region. In Trinidad, after the British colonists banned African slave descendants from playing drums, they resorted to new ways of making music by converting discarded oil drums and inventing the steel pan drum. Today, it is heard throughout the Caribbean in calypso music. In Peru and Bolivia, the unique sounds of the zampona or tarka—Andean pan flutes made from reeds—are easy to recognize. In Colombia, percussion instruments such as maracas made from coconut husks or the guacharaca made from palm tree trunks, set the beat of the nation.

We carry the rhythms of our culture within us and they can remind us of who we are and where we came from. The song of our people is the song of our hearts and if we forget it, we deny a part of ourselves.

◈ ASIMILACIÓN (ASSIMILATION) ◈

"I will listen to the rhythm of my life."

Feel the ancient human experience of song by making music a part of each day. Sing, listen, dance, watch a video, play an instrument or keep the beat with your hands.

◈ AL REVÉS (UPSIDE DOWN) ◈

How have you forgotten to hear the music in life?

37 ✦ BAILE ✦ DANCE

The cumbia is an expressive and soulful dance that was originally a courtship ritual performed by slaves and has become synonymous with Colombian culture. Traditional dancers are barefoot, and their costumes are reminiscent of the Afro-Colombian roots of the dance. The tribal drums set the mood and viewers can't help shaking their hips or tapping their feet when a good cumbia is performed. The limbo originated in Trinidad and Tobago but is now a party favorite around the world. It was a West African tradition performed at wakes to symbolize the crossing over from one world to the next. But like the tango, mambo, salsa and merengue, these dances have become part of mainstream culture because immigrants have brought their celebratory dances with them through the centuries.

Humans have always found a way to express themselves through dance and movement and each country and region has its individual way of moving. These bailes can tell stories, transform our pain and convey our emotions.

⬖ ASIMILACIÓN (ASSIMILATION) ⬖

"I honor the dance of life."

Remember to move your body and dance, even if just for a moment. If you are not able to move or dance, watch a video of dancers. What makes your spirit dance?

⬖ AL REVÉS (UPSIDE DOWN) ⬖

What is preventing you from loosening up or being a little carefree? When was the last time you danced?

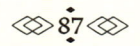

38 ◆ DISFRAZO ◆ COSTUME

The parade at the Oruro festival in Bolivia is a spectacle to behold! The holiday was originally celebrated by indigenous people to honor their gods. Spanish settlers later incorporated Christian traditions and finally, local miners added their folklore. The combination of these disparate elements creates a whimsical and bizarre mix of thousands of costumed characters beginning with the parade leader, the Archangel Michael, followed by Lucifer and all of his demons who dance the diabladas (devil dances). Other costumed characters included are local animals, the Earth Mother, Pachamama and a variety of bat-like devil gods with elaborate masks and beaded capes.

We all wear a costume of sorts. Having a persona can be a healthy way of sharing part of who we are while protecting what is vulnerable about us. But always hiding behind a mask can keep us from contributing to the experience of fully being ourselves.

◈ ASIMILACIÓN (ASSIMILATION) ◈

"I can choose how I share myself with the world."

Think about the costume you wear. How does your persona serve to protect you or convey something about you? Do you need to revise your costume or change it as you grow?

◈ AL REVÉS (UPSIDE DOWN) ◈

Are you hiding behind a costume that does not suit you?

39 ♦ ARTESANÍAS ♦ CRAFTS

Even before written language existed, early people communicated through simple images that were incorporated into pottery, textiles and other crafts.

Immigrants bring parts of their lives with them wherever they go, like the smell of the ocean, the sound of the symphony of tree frogs at night, or the exact color of the hibiscus in abuela's yard. These memories spill out beautifully into their handmade ceramics and crafts.

There is a catharsis to bringing a memory to life by making something with our hands. It creates a mind and body connection and gives us a concrete, visual representation to hold on to.

◈ ASIMILACIÓN (ASSIMILATION) ◈

"I can use my hands to create beauty in the world."

What special memories do you have from where you grew up that wake up your senses? Is there a traditional craft from your culture that you can learn? If you are not crafty, buy a small handmade item from your culture to place on your altar or in a prominent place in your home.

◈ AL REVÉS (UPSIDE DOWN) ◈

Are you in your head too much? How can you bring your memories and thoughts into reality?

40 ✦ JUEGOS ✦ GAMES

At any given time, a fútbol match can be seen being played in the streets throughout Latin America. Latinx people work hard, but they definitely know how to play and have fun too. Even the early people of Colombia knew this when they invented, tejo, a game that is still widely popular today. Similar to Bocce Ball, the aim is to throw the tejo, a heavy, puck-like disc, towards a clay platform and hit a bull's eye amidst triangle targets with small explosives that go off if you hit them. A tamer version is sapo, a Peruvian game based on an Incan legend about a guardian toad in Lake Titicaca. The goal is to throw gold coins into a toad's mouth. There are always fun and inexpensive diversions to blow off steam with friends at the end of the day.

Playing all the time can be disruptive to our journey, but we need to have moments of leisure to stay healthy and give our brain a break. Plugging into the playful spirit within can help us feel replenished and ready to get back on our camino.

ASIMILACIÓN (ASSIMILATION)

"I choose to play and see the fun side of life."

How can you be more playful? What can you do to make more time for play in your life?

AL REVÉS (UPSIDE DOWN)

When is the last time you made time to play? Are you taking yourself or life too seriously?

41 ◆ DIVERSIDAD ◆ DIVERSITY

There are new species of flora and fauna being discovered in the Amazon rainforest approximately every two days. Colombia alone is home to more orchid species than any other country and is the second-largest exporter of flowers in the world. Just this year, new species of frogs have been identified in the Andean forests and in Peru, there are over four thousand varieties of potatoes. Our planet is bountiful and filled with mysteries. With each discovery, we learn more about our environment and ourselves.

Humans embrace diversity in nature, but we are less tolerant of differences between people.

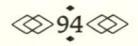

There are treasures to be discovered in each one of us and these differences are worth celebrating because they are what make us special and enhance our lives.

◈ ASIMILACIÓN (ASSIMILATION) ◈

"I open myself to exploring the mysteries within."

What sets you apart? Is there a physical attribute, talent or ability that you have forgotten to pay attention to? How can you find a way to use your differences to your advantage?

◈ AL REVÉS (UPSIDE DOWN) ◈

Are you hiding your differences or viewing them as flaws?

42 ◆ SIESTA ◆ NAP

You can forget about your schedule when visiting most Latin American countries. Time runs a little slower, service takes a bit longer and if you have errands to run between noon and two p.m. you will probably have to wait because most businesses will be closed for siesta. It might seem irresponsible to waste two full hours of daylight, but it is more than a nap. It is a designated time to enjoy a leisurely lunch and be with family, even if you are not actually napping.

Sometimes, we need a reminder to slow down and dedicate time to rest and recharge our batteries. As long as the break is a reprieve and not a way of avoiding the task-at-hand, it can help us be more productive.

ASIMILACIÓN (ASSIMILATION)

"I choose to make time to rest my mind, body and spirit."

What can you do to rest your physical body and your mind today? Can you find a regular time during your day to rest, even if for ten minutes?

AL REVÉS (UPSIDE DOWN)

Have you been napping too long and avoiding what needs to be done?

43 ◆ FIESTA ◆ PARTY

It's no secret that Latinx people do not need an excuse to party or have a parade. In fact, Brazil, Colombia and Trinidad boast some of the biggest Carnaval celebrations in the world, where music, dancing, costumes and festivities take over daily life for weeks. It is a time to be joyful and let loose before the somber season of Lent begins.

Too much partying can be hazardous to our health and relationships, but it is important to make time to celebrate and be among the living. Even during dark and difficult times, we can choose to acknowledge the good things worth raising our cup for.

⬥ ASIMILACIÓN (ASSIMILATION) ⬥

"I celebrate the joy of being alive."

Where can you find joy around you? How can you celebrate life more fully? Celebrate small occasions. Toast to a warm day, a good friendship or your health.

⬥ AL REVÉS (UPSIDE DOWN) ⬥

Have you become too introverted or isolated? Have you been reluctant to celebrate or find reasons to enjoy life?

44 • ÉXITO • SUCCESS

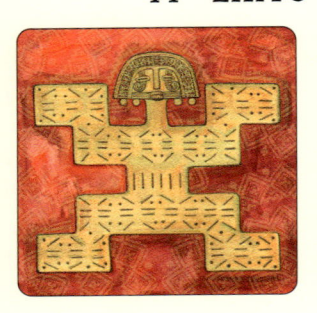

The jaguar was revered by tribes in the Amazon as a symbol of strength and power. As the apex predator, it was both feared and respected and frequently represented in masks, ceramics and textiles. To achieve our goals and attain success of any kind, we sometimes need to channel our inner jaguar energy. While our human worth is not defined by our successes or accomplishments, acknowledging these milestones or reaching specific goals should be celebrated.

But becoming power hungry and obsessed with the idea of success can be a misdirection. Success is not the destination, but merely a stop on the path to prepare for the next leg of the journey. Looking back on our travels is a way of measuring the progress we have made so far.

◈ ASIMILACIÓN (ASSIMILATION) ◈

"I have traveled far on my journey and take this moment to enjoy the rewards."

Recognize how far you have come and the power you have within that got you here. Take a moment to view your progress and acknowledge your successes and the strength it took to achieve them.

◈ AL REVÉS (UPSIDE DOWN) ◈

Are you only focusing on how far you have to go rather than where you are now? Are you feeling powerless?

BIOGRAPHY

Sabina Espinet is a multi-cultural artist and a first-generation Colombian immigrant based in Colorado. She is interested in our shared divine connection and has illustrated other card decks for U.S. Games, *Mudras for Awakening the Energy Body, Mudras for Awakening the Five Elements* and *Auspicious Symbols.* To see more of her art visit www.sabinaespinet.com

ACKNOWLEDGEMENTS

Gracias! This deck is dedicated to my ancestors and the lessons they teach me daily about resilience. Especially my Colombian abuela, Clara. When she was fifteen, she was told by her mother that it was time to marry, so she chose the kindest of her suitors and immigrated to Trinidad where she didn't speak the language or know anyone, but still managed to raise eight children.

I am also grateful for the constant flow of love from my husband, John and my children, Max and Madeline who listen to all of my ideas and support me every step of the way in everything I attempt.

And a special thank you to the U.S. Games team for taking a chance on me, especially Lynn Araujo for seeing something in me and pushing me out of the nest on this project and Alison DeNicola for always encouraging me to fly. You are both remarkable, inspiring women and I am grateful for your friendship and collaboration.

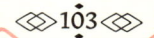

A quick primer on Sabina's native country
COLOMBIA

Colombia is named after the Italian conquistador, Christopher Columbus (Cristóbal Colón in Spanish, hence the spelling with two o's). Like many South American countries, it celebrates a richly layered ethnic background made up of indigenous people, European settlers and African descendants, all of whom have influenced the broader culture.

It is geographically diverse, bordered by both the Pacific and Atlantic Oceans and the Amazon River and is bisected by the Andes Mountains.

Notable Colombians include: Nobel prize author, Gabriel García Márquez; artist, Fernando Botero; singer, Shakira; artist/activist/musician, Lido Pimienta; fashion editor, Nina Garcia; actors, John Leguizamo and Sofia Vergara and many fútbol athletes like, Willington Ortiz and Carlos Valderrama.

USA
MEXICO
The BAHAMAS
CUBA
HAITI
DOMINICAN REPUBLIC
BELIZE
JAMAICA
PUERTO RICO
ANTIGUA & BARBUDA
HONDURAS
DOMINICA
GUATEMALA
NICARAGUA
ST. VINCENT & THE GRENADINES
ST. LUCIA
BARBADOS
EL SALVADOR
GRENADA
PANAMA
TRINIDAD & TOBAGO
COSTA RICA
VENEZUELA
GUYANA
SURINAME
FRENCH GUYANA
COLOMBIA
ECUADOR
BRAZIL
PERU
BOLIVIA
PARAGUAY
CHILE
URUGUAY
ARGENTINA

⋙ MY CAMINO ⋘

Use the space on the next few pages to write about your journey, ancestors, or to design your own flag spread.

Here are some journaling prompts to help you define your journey.

- Where have I come from and where do I want to go in life?
- Which ancestors inspire me the most to get to my destination?
- What events in my own life have brought me to this point?
- How am I healing and getting back on my path more each day?
- When I get sidetracked, what are the forks in the road that I can choose?
- In what ways can I creatively express my camino?

For our complete line of tarot decks, books, meditation cards, oracle sets, and other inspirational products please visit our website:

www.usgamesinc.com

Stay connected with us!

U.S. GAMES SYSTEMS, INC.
179 Ludlow Street • Stamford, CT 06902 USA
Phone: 203-353-8400 • Order Desk: 800-544-2637
FAX: 203-353-8431